abductions

ABDUCTIONS

poems by
chiwan choi

writ large press
los angeles

ISBN: 9780981483634

Cover art by Nathan Ota & Risk, entitled "Riskone"
Book design by Judeth Oden Choi

Published by:
writ large press
Los Angeles, CA
writlargepress.com

Table of Contents

for us

the fires across

we walked up to the rooftop
of our apartment in bushwick,
carrying a new bottle of chinese whiskey
that a friend brought back
from her trip to beijing.

it was fourth of july
and we wanted to see the fireworks across
the water.

we were still in our sleep clothes—
pajama pants
or sweat pants,
something with elastic.

i remember this because
it was so easy to put my hand down her pants
and grab her ass
as a couple of neighbors,
who'd also come up to see the festivities,
stood by trying not to stare.

i took the first swig
and passed her the bottle,
a jug right out of a saturday afternoon
kung-fu movie
with badly dubbed english.

she twisted her face
because the whiskey tasted so bad

like medicine my parents
brewed in a crock pot
that we referred to as deer antler juice.

then we watched, the four of us,
and there was emotion, i think,
judy telling me how much she loved
the fourth of july,

the tears soon after
as she couldn't help but remember
her first week at nyu grad,
how they ran outside
then toward uptown
as the towers came down.

i remembered something too—
there were two of us standing there,
a different two of us on a different rooftop,
this one in los angeles
on gramercy drive near 9th street,

our small hands on the cold bricks
that rose waist high,
and i held out the last watermelon now & later
toward her without turning
and i felt her fingers
on the palm of my right hand
as she scooped it away.

i listened
to the unwrapping,

to the slight breath as she opened her mouth,
unaware that she was a sacrifice,
to her teeth sticking
in the chewy pink candy with her first bite,
and i closed my eyes
to feel the breeze against my face
without interruption,
remaining still
as i heard two more things—

her shoes scraping against the top of the wall
and that last grunt.

and when it was silent again,
i opened my eyes to find myself alone,
that smell of ash that remains after each loss,
the wrapper fluttering on the ground
an inch from my shoe.

it is the opening line of a song—
on a rooftop in brooklyn—
a song that is not mine
but this moment will become etched
eternally,

this moment
of a decision that i will make:
to hide my secrets from her
to not tell her about the history of my family
to not share with her
even one story about the night lights
and the disappearances—

3.

hoping,
on the rooftop
with the bottle of chinese whiskey
that can't fix me,
the fires on the other side of the water,
unable to make the year stay
no matter how much i dig my fingers
into her skin,
that she won't mind
losing everything she ever wanted
to spend a few
listless
and unforgettable years
together.

dulce de leche

it was my first week of school
in paraguay,
at nuestra señora de perpetuo socorro,
learning another new language
in the middle of south america.

i hadn't started school yet in korea
before we were all taken again
and dropped here,
where the northern half of the country
was still undeveloped jungle.

it was all new—
the language
the school
the nuns
the uniforms.

one afternoon,
a classmate brought something her mother had made.
it was in a jar and it looked like melted caramel.
i stared at it with my mouth open
and she told me what it was.

when i came home,
still in my white shirt and blue shorts,
the black shoes i'd just learned to tie on my own,
i ran into the bathroom and leaned against the sink,
face close to the mirror
so i could watch my lips move,

repeating the words,
"dulce de leche,"
over and over,
frightened that words that i didn't understand
could make my body tremble and burn.

the send off

they were trying to send me off
to my relatives on the east coast for the summer.
this is what the children of normal families did,
what their parents encouraged.

i stood next to my father,
who was on the phone
sitting at the dining room table,
and i waved my hands in the air,
silently mouthing "no, no,"
not even stopping to wipe
the tears falling down my face.

he stared at me,
motioned for me to stop crying,
then pointed toward my room.

i ran from him
past the television in the living room,
upsetting my brother who was watching
benny hill slapping his old bald sidekick.

i went into the room i shared with my brother
and after locking the door,
i leaned against it,
the crying turning to a whimper.

i was tired.
i didn't want to be taken away again.
i just wanted a normal life,
to be with my family.

all i heard was dad laughing on the phone,
while talking to his sister in new york,
as i turned off the light in my room.
i shuffled my feet
over the carpet toward the window,
pushed the frayed curtain an inch
with my left hand,
and watched my neighbor getting ready to go out,
her purple panty shiny
against her dark black skin.

fishing

we left our parents at the pier
because it was freezing,
but they kept at it,
mom laughing each time she felt
the line bite into her finger.
they were using fishing lines
wrapped around empty coke cans
because we hadn't gone to sears yet
to buy our first fishing poles.

margaret and i were both 11 years old.
we didn't care about fish.
i didn't even like eating fish.
all we knew was that
we could hear our teeth chatter out there
and all that bait cutting was nasty.

we crawled into the back
of the blue toyota pick-up ,
hoping the vista camper shell
would shield us from the cold.
i started staring at her cleavage.
i couldn't help it; it was like a tracking beam.
her breasts were already legendary at school
and the boys gave me a hard time
because they knew
she and i were next-door neighbors.
she looked up at me
and wrapped her arms around her chest
to cover herself—

this is what she did everyday
to shield herself from all the men,
her dad
her brother
neighbors
and teachers.

and now me, this boy trembling next to her,
and i tried to make conversation
about bisons and other dead things,
telling her about the ghost in my childhood home
who used to sit on the steps
and about the UFOs in paraguay
and the artifacts my father kept
inside the piano chair.

then she smiled
and moved her left leg over
until it touched my right,
her arms falling back to her sides,
turning any words i had left to speak
into sounds i couldn't spell.

lovers

we were on my bed,
on our sides facing each other,
curled up so that our knees touched
as the smiths record spun on the sansui turntable
that my brother bought out of anger.

and i reached out
and touched the knuckles of her left hand
as she pointed at the scar
on my forehead,
wanting to know
how i got that strange mark.

we didn't hear the door open
when my father walked in,
pausing to watch us for a few seconds
at me, his youngest son,
trying to find his way
into the beginning of a life
that didn't contain the one he gave to me.

i don't know how long he'd been there
when i finally looked up,
but we made eye contact
and a smile that lasted only a second
before he wagged his finger
and he walked out,
closing the door quietly behind him.

the tip of her finger
came closer to my face,
touching my scar, tracing it down
to my wet temple.
she started to ask
but all she could get out was why,
and i jumped out of bed,
lifted the needle to place it back at the start.

i couldn't turn back around
even as her knees made a sound against my blanket,
even though for once there was a noise
in this room like breathing.
and as 'reel around the fountain' began
i sang out loud,
one day it will be time for my tale to be told.

she laughed
and told me we are both so young and stupid
and she got out of bed, stood behind me close,
making the fuzz on the back of my neck shift.
i turned around and faced her,
to remind myself why i wasn't supposed to know her
and her touch was on my face again,
her fingerprints slipping on the wet surface of my skin,
as my father called my name from below,
now safely away from here,
and i asked her
if it was already time for her to go.

what i wanted to write

during lunch all through senior year in high school,
i sat alone in the hallway,
empty except an occasional student
walking past and trying hard not to stare at me
and a japanese man
who taught karl marx every year
waiting for his class by the door.

one morning,
while hanging out with the guys
i'd grown up with since fifth grade—
listening to them complain about
bitches who wouldn't suck dick
and their moms not giving them money
and comparing new kenwood pullouts
that they stole—
i stood up,
told them how much i hated them all,
how i was never going to sit there with them again.

it was some serious teen angst melodrama
but i just couldn't do it anymore,
listen to them droning on
about their simple uninterrupted lives
while i had to remain silent,
tell nobody about us,
about the scars that appear
on my body that doctors can't explain.

if i was to be silent,
i wanted to be alone.

at nights,
i sat in my room,
staring at the stains and cracks on the ceiling,
my brother's bed next to mine
empty for the past year,
bracing for the next time,
each night bracing for the next time.

until one night i looked
in the closet
and found my brother's old typewriter
that he'd bought
for the sole purpose of writing a paper
on *The Human Comedy.*

and i started to write too,
more than mere paper,
to turn my life into evidence
of the things i held in my skin,
falling asleep each night
with my face on the keys
of the sears electric typewriter,
my room smelling of the markers I was sniffing,
blood stains on the wall by the door
around the light switch
reminders of the desperation in darkness,
the sheet of paper curled around the drum of the machine
praying for words to appear;

as downstairs my mother continued to knit
another blanket to cover
the parts of our family
that were unprotected—

father's blood,
her own cold aging legs.

abduction

this time the winter of 74, a year before we left.
it was always winter in that place i can't quite recall.
but i have spoken of this before,
of the time i wandered through the nameless streets
in seoul, paper money crumpled tight in my right hand,
the tips of the fingers of my left hand sliding on the surface
of walls and steel gates; trying not to lose contact
because it is this thing that touches my skin in daylight
that guides me home, this surface until the end
where i lost myself at the fallen snow.

the point is not that my mother found me,
as i cried in the alley behind the house,
but the details i have so far left out—that my father
was at work again, building a ramp up to the church
a cab ride away, where grandmother would later
plant rosebushes and name them after her grandsons,
my namesake the one second to the left—
my brother and i would run to them each sunday morning,
up the zig-zag of the concrete ramp that father would
eventually finish, to stand in front of them, comparing
the growth, how i waited for my name to grow taller
than the world as i pulled at the sleeve of mother's blouse.

nor is the point the cracks on the asphalt that appeared
after the snow to swallow the regrets of a city in january
as a voice abducted me around the bends.

this is not the lie i expected—
an attempt to put into words

the sparrow that kept returning each morning
to our balcony and our sunlight,
promising us a child, a daughter,
leaving a note with the name we were to give her.
how do i speak of these things?

i am now what remains of the details i choose to cherish
as i join my family once a month
and we do what we always have done to bare it,
tell each other new stories of ghosts
and shadows that we can't explain,
as mother entwines her short fingers
and tells us that one, that story,
about the ocean and the waves rising like cypresses
and the spaceship that has come for her
since she was a child.

when it is my turn,
i tell them i have been staying up nights,
my wife asleep next to me with her arms above her head,
and i tell them about all the UFOs over argentina
until he smiles, his mouth smaller now over his dentures.
"did i tell you about the chilean soldiers
who witnessed the spaceships before the war
with argentina broke out?" he asks.
"yes, about the invisible dragons," i say.
he nods, happy that i have once again embraced
the unseen guides that lead me to rapture.

but see, even here, it's those things i leave out—
i don't even begin to tell them about that sunday
at the emergency room,

walking through the hallways,
my fingers touching the surface of things,
of tables and curtains, of walls and telephones,
to find her there, sitting on a metal bed,
somewhere between laughing and crying,
the sparrow having come and gone with what it had gifted,
my left hand on her thigh covered in worn denim,
my right one in a fist around a crumpled name.

in between

first the war
then comes the dying in separate rooms
of an apartment filled with dust

in between—

the brown bottle on broadway and ord

the tuesday morning
with the singing neighbor

chair spinning
in an almost empty room

her breath on my palm
that feels like a word

freezing myself so i can wake up

mother's silk scarf blowing off her hair
on a january morning

leaning the seat back
to catch the weight of our weeks

getting lost behind fedco

how i tried to remember everyone
by their scent.

salvation

on the northwest corner
of 7th and broadway at 7:45am,
i wait by the newspaper stand
where i buy
my double A batteries.
across 7th
they are already out,
the street preachers
witnessing in spanish.

there are sometimes different ones on each corner—

a korean teen, because koreans are nothing if not subtle,
holding a giant sign over his head proclaiming
god says read bible or die!;
sometimes a black man with a nice hat
on the northeast corner
a few yards from clifton's cafeteria;
a couple of white boys now and again,
in white shirts and black ties.

i call this salvation corner
and i walk through it each morning with my dog,
back and forth, between 7 and 8am.

when we first moved down here,
judy looked at the sign on the marquee
outside the old state theater,
where now instead of movies they have church,
and she said,

'jesus christ is the mister,'
and pointed.
i read it too—
jesucristo es el señor—
and nodded
and we repeated this to each other,
jesus christ is the mister,
our mantra for the rest of the week.

and at 9:06am,
i drink last night's wine,
bitter and warm,
looking at the phone when it lights up.
it tells me
bad bad people want all my money
because that's how i've added
all the collection agency numbers into my address book
so i could assign them a silent ringtone.

this is how it begins:

another day's waiting
for the sparrows to return to our balcony,
where we found them when we first moved in
for death
for salvation
for cancer
for a heart attack
for broken corner jesuses.

the ending goes like this:

she is standing by the dresser i found in the hallway,
thrown away by another tenant that lost his job
and had to move.

naked,
the bruise on her left arm from our last fight
is exposed about an inch below her shoulder,
the fight that left my right index finger with torn ligaments
and the nightshirt she's owned since 12
ripped to pieces on the floor.

that night of tequila
and trying not to talk about my leg that keeps breaking,
trying not to talk about our fractured marriage,
trying not to talk about our baby gone;

all that's not spoken of coming out
in screams
and punches
and spit—
the dog hiding under the desk.

we are drunk again,
what's left of the open wine bottles souring on the table.
we crawl into bed.
we have switched sides so i can be by the window
where the cold air slips in through the cracks.

i lick her neck
until it smells like grapes.

'so drunk,' she says

soon she is snoring
and whimpering in her sleep
and i place my hand on her stomach,
tell that place
i am ready,
i am ready now,
until i fall asleep.

at 4:15am,
we are both awake again in the dark.
she can't sleep when the alcohol wears off
and i can't sleep when she is drowning.

'you okay?' i ask

'yeah,' she says. 'drank too much.'

'i'll make fish soup tomorrow,' i say

'ok,' she says.

'ok,' i say.

alarm

in the dark
i lie still
my eyes blinking at the ceiling

she sleeps
with her back to me
trying to find her own warmth

at 6
the alarm will sound
but it will be mere static

because
the dial keeps moving
to a space between stations

and i will
fumble for her
our sick mouths dry against each other

as i try
to stay hard
as she tries to stay awake

and we will
both fail and return to the waiting
for the static to signal

something.

plots

we return to their apartment
on lafayette park place,
the one with the heater
my parents can't use
because it's too old
and it kicks out dust
that aggravates my father's allergy.

we have spent another morning
filling out applications for senior housing,
25 pages each this time
for my mom and dad.

i sat between them,
swiveling back and forth to translate
and point at the proper line
where the signature goes,
and laughed when my father
pointed at the question
that wanted to know
if he'd ever run a meth lab
in his previous home.

and now we are
in their apartment
that is too small
and too hot
and too expensive.

we are joined by my brother robert

and my wife judy
and i catch mom peeking
at judy's belly,
hoping to see it grow once more
as she walks into the kitchen
to grab a pear to slice.

i take a seat on the floor
at judy's feet
as mom comes out of the kitchen
with the plate
and five tiny forks
and dad hands robert his bottle
of blood pressure medicine
that robert's been taking
since he quit his job,

and i tell them,
as we sit in some misshapen circle,
that michel's grandfather passed away
but he left 600 thousand dollars
for each of his daughters
and now michel's mother is rich,
and mom says,
waaaaahhhh,
and takes another glimpse
at judy's belly,
still waiting for that thing to name.

and my father clears his throat
and says,
i got news for you!

he says,
remember those two burial plots we bought
five years ago
at rose hills,
the ones off to the side
that were just being developed?
and mom says,
by the flowers
by the water
by the road?
and he says,
remember those?

i nod,
squeeze judy's foot with my right hand,

and he says,
we bought two and paid 800 bucks for each
and now they're worth 20,000 per plot.

20,000?

20,000, robert says.

and dad leans back on the couch and begins to laugh
and mom smiles
and robert rubs his own growing stomach

and dad begins to clap
and soon we all join in
and we are laughing
and he gets up

and grabs the liquor he's been making
on the balcony
from honey and persimmon,
his medicinal moonshine,
and he pours it for all of us
and lifts his cup,

and dad says,
to wealth!
to our wealth!

and mom says,
to our wealth!

and robert says,
to our wealth!

and judy says,
to our wealth!

and i say,
to our wealth!

on fire, oh god

the sun just came out like a minute ago.
it's almost 1pm.
staring out the window, it's actually pretty.
it's blue with nice clouds,
although i learned it's not really blue
the first time i visited north carolina.
those people will tell you, their sky is blue.
i can't argue, but this is what i know.
what i see above me and what it's been for 30 years now.
this is the sky i know.

there are three manuscripts waiting for me
to read and mark up.
i pour myself a glass of malbec from last night.
it's not very good but it's wine.
i don't think i want to read these manuscripts today.
i'll work on the mahfouz novel instead.
i think he has written one of my favorite lines.
the first sentence of chapter 2.
"i am on fire, oh god."
you can't write a better sentence.

the dog just woke up.
she scratches herself on the right ear,
then jumps on our bed.
it is hard to see all the hair she leaves behind
on the gold duvet cover judy bought at ikea.
we notice it at night
when we're trying to sleep,
our bodies rolling to and from each other,

legs kicked out from underneath the cover,
and the dog hair flies up and covers our faces,
leaving us spitting in the dark.

we are not pregnant again this month.
she got home yesterday
while i was washing dishes
and i asked her whether her students liked
watching romeo & juliet
and how the grammy museum was
and i was scrubbing dried tomato sauce off a white plate
when she looked at me
and i held my hands in the warm running water
and she said her period started
and she cried.

and i knew, i knew all day
because my stomach was hurting
and i realized i needed to go buy ice cream
because we would need ice cream.

and she was crying while eating it
and watching bones on tv
and i told her how my stomach hurt all day
and that i would be crying too later,
later before bed.
she nodded and kept eating the ice cream
before it melted
and we changed the channel,
found out about the ancient aliens,
and i pointed at the ruins in peru,

told her that those were the pictures my dad showed me
when i was 4,
stopping short of telling her the reason,
how he was trying to help me understand
what was happening to our family.

i tried to put my arm around her
and caught my thumb in her shirt sleeve
and i cringed because it still hurt.
i think there is something torn in my right wrist.
it is better than a month ago,
but still not back to normal.
i don't think it will ever heal.
i keep going back to my doctor
but each time, the last four times,
he refuses to stick needles in me.
he makes me sit and read a book while he cleans his office.
he smiles at me during lunch without a word.
he just nods when i say i am frustrated with my body.

and when i squirm on the couch,
my wrist hurting so bad,
he only says,
"why do you insist your body remember all the pain?"
and smiles again.
he is breaking me but i can't tell him the truth,
how i hurt it one night
while trying to kill my wife in a rage,
fragments returning a week later—
of her body flying across the room,
and the bruises,

one on her arm, one by her clavicle,
all making me return to the scene.

"maybe they really were aliens," she said
as i cringed, holding my hand
as she cried again
because we were still not pregnant.

i feel like there were a bunch of things
i was supposed to do today.
it is quiet.
i am on fire, oh god.
oh god.

i think i'll call my mom after i finish this glass,
see how she's recovering from her surgery,
tell her what they need to get ready
to give to the leasing office.
i got them a low-income unit in our building,
one floor down.
people ask me if i'm crazy
to want my parents so close.
i tell them perhaps,
but it's just that
i want to know what happens,
when the sun begins to set,
if we all gather together,
close,
in silence.

battle in heaven

we use our hands
sick
and
trembling
to reattach
our bodies to each other

touching
the surface of one face
then
the other
the dare to need
more
to love
more

and
we say
that we miss us
in a different city
where
we once killed hunger
with champagne
and
sex on the platform
while waiting
for the L train

then
each of us

face the other way
to fight our way to sleep
battle in silence
for what
we once promised
ourselves
we'd find.

sweet potatoes

she tells me to come down
and wait for her
so she can drop off
baked sweet potatoes
on her way to church

i stand in the courtyard
coughing
and a neighbor walks past
with her dog
that pulls hard toward me

i lean down to pet her
as mom comes around the corner
in her sunday outfit
a little brown paper bag
in her hand

and she smiles
from a distance
waving her free hand
as the dog sniffs my shoe

she calls out
'bella!'
mistaking the dog
for mine

and when she is close enough
she shakes her head

disappointed at her mistake
holding the bag out
for me

and i turn
wave over my shoulder
walk away fast
trying not to think
of the day

she will no longer recognize me
she will mistake me
for a past she can't recall.

the break of the line

this skin of my skin,
shield from embrace and wonder—
invisible stains, the barrier of winds,
weight and weightlessness—
holding me in the eclipse
of light and transfiguring
in mute, in third, in felt.

i rush
at the gate and the red horizon,
you speaking to me
in loud mornings of fading mountains
or the peaks that claim
the light of the living.

the sky turned
to canvas, paint caught
in colors of sheer madness,
three layers above the fence,
above the rust of the railing
holding me suspended,
above the courtyard
and flames, the ficus, glass doors.

i am the lost battle
of a hillside prayer, the rock
clutched into shards;
i am the closed fist of my heart
flickering the face of god,
drawn in crayons,

point to point,
edge to edge.

i ignite the pages
with my lips
and toss them into the center,
the backward sway
of remembering and regret
waits for autumn
to come from the ashes of the west.

what is storm—
to be said but only from the shelter,
to mean that i am descending
upon the cages of mercy and briar;
to squeeze it
until it means to,
before the completion of the light.

the sureness
of walls that burn
forging these blades in my arms,
the new horizons that bleed
i claim as mine—
the places that i have held,
the places that needed
my grip.

how it comes,
as promised, not with an avalanche
of bones, but simply
a hole in her eye—how i hear it

calling her name with a broken line
cradled in a sea of symmetry
and light diffused. the constant
disruption of the water's surface
sits still, eternal, hidden
from view as it is
on the curved end of the turn.

of two weeks ago
after 68 years centered
between the dead and the lost,
roots begging out of the ground,
these fingers counting that way.
they are not always searching
through the blindness
of orchids wilting; we, fabric
draped on sticks to dry,
colors imagined, are.

in the stillness
she finds knees unscathed
by the rocks that catch,
the sleep on thursday
terrified of it. age progresses
until it changes, becomes that season
of falling and frozen,
how it freezes inside
the expectations of bones,
of simple angles
and straight lines.

she wanted to catch
the light beyond rays
slicing thin across the heavy table,
reaching for the water lighter
than the dust,
to the proximity of origin—
the first air born of divine,
and she counted from the left-most,
that one off the wall, deliberate
in the joy of each number,
until that one, that one
above the AC,
breaking.

the stillness
is this—what hopes
in darkness, not to mean
in what is broken, rather, simply,
places without light—
this surrounding atmosphere
over the black couch worn well.
those hands on those knees
peeking above a housedress,
merely lifted,
in intervals without order,
to reach for the invisible things
that fix.

it is not long but soon
she finds them in the lines
where the walls meet,
the makeshift bookshelf of creaky steel,

a silver frame in need of polish
holding the stagnancy
of a man playing soccer,
in her own line that hovers
in the air before her,
drawn with a quiet finger—
encased in lines that no longer follow
the rules.

falling is
the snow impossibly inside
the fragments that search
for the fire in unheard places,
a cratered garden, a woman
in transition, hand parting
her short hair to the right,
melting into a different form
of itself that fits into her fists,
clenched around the screaming
birth of faith.

she straightens out her shoulders
to find acceptance in a statuary
as she counts her blessings backwards.
the end is to be
what begins from now,
the majesty of fabric
stitched with her own hands,
the thumb punctured through with a needle
but like everything at this end,
the beginning, clean.

and in the stale air
of fried squid and antlers
and roots cooked in pots
made for festivities,
she sees the son that she remembers to love,
the one hiding behind the plant
too large for the space that holds
the end of her life, the blue vase
gathered from the corner of the street,
the son whose lines
have always been broken,
even before the evidence
appeared in her eye.

that chant
to the tune of a wartime whimper
of her youth,
the anger in her father's face,
calling out to him, him,
who hesitates out from behind the plant
to stand before her until she sees
the breaks in his legs.

this is how
you fall, she says,
this is how you fall—
asking god to translate his words
and all the scribbles on broken skin
and those etched in exposed bones,
fractured into submission,
teeth gnashed in that last of hope
transcribed into scripture.

she, together
with the son and the spirit,
the makeshift tv stand tilting to the right,
breaking everything
into the tiniest fragments,
the unpronounceable names of divinity,
her son's poetry without rhymes—
and motionless on the couch,
she snaps them, all the lines
that break around her,
until the pieces are, like her,
too small to hold the coming
of death.

this is where
she battles godliness—hiding
its torn hem in the dark corners
or clutching or holding
or praying hands honoring
victory and loss with something less
cliché than a sigh—a frozen pose,
this thing of stoicism.
the silence of the cup on the coffee table
and the unrelenting stillness
of her feet in blue slippers.

was the sacrifice
once believed to have been made
in a past winter with a yes? oh,
to have thought after deliberation
that the worth is in the saving
of form, simple as the act of seeing!

plans stitched into the fabric
covering generations of fathers,
to own for the sake of hiding
the plane surface of the beauty of secrets—
the leather beneath her slow to warm
while breaking into the shape
of all that had broken within.

oh mother,
sister, woman of silence,
how she feared the water
and the cycle of incoming and outgoing,
that tide calling her
from the froth at her toes—
how could it have been possible
to understand that
what she had been carrying inside
since the night on a wooden boat,
flat on her back, the night
where the explosions in the sky that made her
feel like a child weren't explosions at all,
but fate and dying and salvation
in long travelled light.

said to be covered
in skin that will not age,
loved for her stature that can exist in mere shadows,
only heard from once that night
in the back room
tied in ropes before she could choose—
this space that greets her feet
curling and uncurling,

this time the break appearing
where the ceiling remains suspended
above the off center metal shelving,
how her mouth wants
to form a word that describes it.

but the mornings, unfurled,
the routine of darkness and cold—
of finding the invisible christ
to wrap around her cold shoulders.
the pulsing—frozen—
hunger masqueraded into prayer requests—
joy of what's to come, quiet
like thieves, as absent
as language and vocabulary—the shape
of winter and rain.

faith, faith to thee,
and phone calls to this son of night
that she leaves like steps
on the packed sand before the tide—
until she finds the word for this
stillness;
the calm of an empty apartment
caught between worlds—
unaware that he, this son,
is changing the narrative—
a pen, a hammer,
repairing her lines that break
with a series
of broken lines.

the hour

when i get off the train
on hope st.
coming back from the doctor's,
i walk into the bar
and find the one empty seat
at the end
below the television.

i shake the bartender's hand
and ask him how things are with his wife
as he pours my beer.
he shrugs,
tells me the divorce will start soon,
and taps the counter twice with his knuckles.

there's a man
from a bank across the street
finishing his happy hour wine
and he's trying to talk
to the two younger men next to me
who look more successful
because their drinks are mixed
and he is asking about hamburgers
and secret bars
and how he swears there were more dogs
dressed for halloween this year
than last.

but the younger ones ignore him
and i teach him how to spell blue

without an e
and my second beer is done
and the barkeep pours me a shot of don julio
and one for himself
because he is still angry.

i take a picture
of an elbow
and a black coated man
and take another shot of tequila
for the road
and walk into the darkness that comes
too early
and walk east,
thinking of the chinaman
telling me i'm losing
my temperature.

at home,
we don't talk.
we lie next to each other
parallel
like chopsticks
as she reads midnight's children
because she can't let me win
like i can't let her live.

the phone rings.
it's my father.
i don't answer.
the phone rings again.
it's mother.

she is frightened
because she can't reach my brother.
it says the phone's not working, she says,
you know he has no money.
he hasn't worked in years.
he has no food.
what do i do, she says.

i tell her not to go.
i tell her not to sneak into his building
and not to knock on his door.
i tell her i will write his life tonight
and in it,
he will be on the couch,
his stomach full
and laughing at seinfeld reruns.
in it
his wife will still be there
and they will have kids,
a dozen like he always wanted.
in it
he will be alive,
breathing
behind that door.
in it
he is listening to brüchner,
smiling as he thinks of me,
how we agreed that
this was a 3rd rate composer.

in it
he buys a house for our family

where tomatoes can grow by the fence
and the soil in the yard will be fertile
and my daughter will still be there
in that yard
long enough
for her to squeeze my thumb
in her hand.

i tell her
this is why i write:

to keep all of us alive
on white sheets of paper,
in combinations
of abstract shapes
with harsh angles,
even those
who have been taken
from us,
one time long ago
and
once more;

to keep us,
not breathing,
but
permanent.

bodyguard

yesterday we buried grandma
who died on friday night
while i sat at my bar
drinking free beer.

there weren't many people not too old
so we scrambled to gather
enough pall-bearers.

after loading the coffin in the hearse
i turned to judy.
hey, i said, that wasn't as heavy as i thought.

i've been sitting here
trying to figure out
why i feel nothing
when my relatives die.

someone said to me
last night,
your mom is an orphan now
and you don't have anymore grandparents.

we are putting these books
in boxes for our move on saturday
across the courtyard into a different unit.

the copy of *wise blood*
lingers in my hands
a little longer than the others

as i remember a woman named flannery
at the bar who asked me what i do.

in the new apartment,
i will write on the typewriter again,
on the blue olivetti i bought last year
for 50 dollars.

and at some point
i will write about the only moment
that mattered yesterday:

standing in the parking lot
of a korean restaurant
on wilshire and wilton
after the reception where a handful
of people dressed in black
ate thin sliced beef in silence,
waiting to separate
to our individual cars;
the sun bright above us,
my mom in the middle of the circle,
black plastic wrap around shades
protecting her eye post-surgery;
that moment where she turned
and glimpsed my father,
still sharp in his black suit,
then as the rest of us stood
without words,
not knowing how to say goodbye,
she pointed at herself with her right thumb
and said in english,

me, boss,
then pointed at my father to say,
he, bodyguard.

finding it out either too early or too late or just in time

there has always been
a reason
to read each poem,
taking more time
on these short lines
than it ever made sense:

we wanted
to catch
the poet
in the act of dying,
caught
between the peeling paint
and a damp wall
within the description
of a past room;

to feel the rush
of defying
the present
we are seeing.

and in the writing:

my face buried
in the words
that have tumbled out
on the pages
as i flipped

the smallest moments
over and over
in my hands,
chopping into fractions
the silence
of a family gathered
around a coffee table
until nothing
can be hidden;

looking
for the starting point
of this end
and
failing
to see
how close i've come
to the fall.

and now eternity

i have been alternating between
lying on the floor a few feet from judy's slippers
and going through two bottles of cheap bitter wine.
my back is covered in dog hair
and the brown skin of peanuts
peeled with trembling fingers.

yesterday a friend told me to not drink anymore
because it makes things worse.
she doesn't understand
i am just trying to breathe
then breathe again after that,
and this is what is helping me now—
the wine
the jack daniels given to me by a student
porn on the screen as i write.

creating ritual,
how i've been wiping the counters
and washing the dishes
and vacuuming the same spots each and every day,
walking the dog through downtown each morning,
the exact route,
crossing the streets on the same intersections,
saying hello to the same people scampering to work
or smoking at the corner,
using the same trash can in front of the library
to throw away her shit,
then running around the corner of flower and 6th
for exactly 30 steps—

how i am taking off my shoes the right foot first
as the dog stares at me
while tied to the door handle,
waiting for her feet to be wiped.

it has now been 8 consecutive nights
judy's had to wake me up,
stop me from screaming in my sleep.
a promise she made me 7 years ago,
my first night spent at her apartment in brooklyn,
the window sill of her tiny room
still coated with the ash
from the twin towers across the water,
how i told her i am afraid to sleep,
that i'd slept 3 hours a night for the past 4 years,
that i am terrified of the dark moments of my life,
and her word
that she'd watch over me through our nights
as i stared at the shelves she'd hung crooked on her walls,
thick art books and skinny plays
stacked and lined on each one without worry.

and she kept her promise through our time
in the top floor of a rundown building in bushwick,
our mattress on the paint speckled floor,
the one from which we'd stare up,
lying naked side by side,
watching the snow fall inside our room
through the cracks in the windows,
that winter it hit zero.

i am again burning in terror,
wanting to rip the yellow skin off,
carve every word that's ever meant anything to me
into the brittle surface of my bones,
punctuate it with an amen in honor of my father,
his belt tightening around his shrinking waist,
his fingers in the pocket of his thin gray jacket
rubbing the dime that will pay for his bus ride
to this son he wants to learn to love.

(did i tell you about the time i went back to korea—
it was in the summer of 89,
how they thought i was japanese
because i was wearing shorts and had a goatee,
how i stayed with my aunt, my dad's sister,
how her face looked like his, how my uncle came over,
dad's little brother,
the one with the diabetes that he can't control,
how he sat on the floor, how we all sat on the floor,
how i was next to him and looking at mom,
how her face contorted remembering the kitchen
she was forced into
at grandma's house the moment she married dad,
how someone grabbed my hand,
how i thought it was my dad
although he was back in los angeles,
how i almost said, dad stop it you're embarrassing me,
but it was him, my uncle,
his hand covered in the skin that we all share—
comfort and recognition.)

i don't know what this is. this ending of things.
i don't know what to call it,
but it is not death.
i notice a bloody spot on the left side of the dog's face,
cut from a toenail that hasn't been trimmed.
i call to her with my two hands held out
in front of my knees,
beg her to walk on this concrete floor beneath us,
to echo those small footsteps into the air,
to wrap me in the small sounds of ordinary
like the folding of shoulders the moment after prayer.
i wipe the blood off with my hands until i am covered in it,
telling her this is waiting,
this is waiting,
this blood is the eternity of words
between the beginning and ending
of a moment that wants permanence.

i take off my shirt,
show the dog the new scars on my chest,
then lay down on the floor again,
remembering how i once thought the pain
was a homing device
so i can find my way back,
the scars my bread crumbs home.
but now—
i am merely falling apart into fractions
while trying to disintegrate before they come,
the new secrets i will hold from my wife
as she continues to save me in the darkness,
trying to find all the details of my life on the sidewalks
and crumbling walls around me—

father's five dollar shoes,
robert's plastic tooth stained purple,
waiting and waiting for somebody
to tell me it's okay now,
that it's too late
to ask to be saved.

what lingers in the dark

it is quiet in here tonight.
it's almost midnight
and right now
there isn't even someone screaming at the bus stop
on the southeast corner of 7th and los angeles.

my wife is asleep.
i can't even remember
if we had another fight today,
if one of us cried today,
if i begged her once more
to kill me.

this computer is the only light.
i am shirtless.
i am checking sports scores
and watching porn
between forgetting
and remembering.

a friend finds me
and sends me a note.

she asks
what lingers in the dark

as i snap the icicles hanging from the balcony,
winter frozen skin breaking,
cocoa burning hazelnut,
glass cracked and whimper beneath,
lips and bones and three years of looking,

and heat,
always the heat somewhere
untouched.

feet bare

as soon as i type these words,
the world around them will disappear
except for two trees
poking out from the snow
silent,

like central park
in winter,
where they say
i will find such peace.

but all there is
is an inexplicable fear
of losing my heart
to the motion of my legs.

last night
at 2am,
i opened my eyes
when i searched for her once more

on the wrong side
of myself—
darkness can't be blamed
for the wanting of wrong directions.

i got up for water,
walking through this
on feet cold on concrete,
thinking of father

who always told us
all ill comes from bare feet
on pavement,
from skin touching winter.

it is here,
father,
and i have forgotten how to cover
my stains.

i have forgotten
what it is i wanted that morning
you sat on the black leather couch
watching the twin towers burn on tv,

as i stood behind you,
the letter in my hand,
wanting you to be proud
10 years too late.

i have forgotten
where i thought
my trees were planted
because they remain silent.

i am losing
my heart
while i flap my arms at the window
trying to measure the distance i've flown.

bunker

i don't know
if everything they told me
is true,
about statues carved in stone
that blinked in the chilean sun,
about grandfather's deal
with the visitors to save the family
as the communists came.

these are questions
i allowed myself to forget in '99,
soon after
mom asked me what
she should do
about the tumor
in her stomach.

it is a monday
for all of us—
sons, fathers,
street sweepers,
to forgotten things
on the pavement,
a box of books,
most of them in tact,
on 7th street.

they only taught me
what was given them,
this ability to spill

inward,
to hold our blood
inside us
in bowls made
from hollowed trees
until the weight
of what survives us
gives us comfort.

he—
my mother too—
wanted me to learn
to keep my eyes
on the ending,
to call death
by a familiar name,
giving me god
so i can embrace it.

how she—
my father also—
held me until
i was able
to release these poems
that cannot
save us,

to whistle down
the street
on the intermittent yellow paint
in the center,
to the fire,

to skeletons of ancestors,
to the disappearing shadows
of a neighbor that stood thinking,
to the glory
of these things
we have not known.

it is monday,
but how can i speak
of the sky,
a blue that isn't blue,
when we are
in the basement food court
of a koreatown mall,
eating spicy burnt rice
from stone bowls,
sitting in these end of days
in this bunker
beneath
the world we have fought
to love
as he keeps himself
from smiling at me,
a bunker that will
not hold forever
but long enough
for her to drop seaweed
on my food
with her wooden chopsticks,
long enough for me
to protest.

rid of us

the old gray toyota
we got from salvage
and that sat in the structure
too far for cold mornings,
covered in dust
and dried red specks of coolant,
words scratched out
on the dirty window by young fingertips,
is now gone.

we are in the middle of getting rid
of everything that we have gathered
that was to make something of us—
furniture
books
cars
bowls
albums that were to hold
photos of a baby in growth—

until we are nothing
but the sound of shoes on the brooklyn sidewalk
as i walked in the night,
the smell of spilled bushmills
on the front of my dj shadow hoodie,
her naked torso at the fourth floor window
as she waited to sleep.

distance

3:38am
trying to say good night
to the dark

sometimes there is breathing
in this room

3:38am
someone is singing
at the bus stop

i'd like to take
a picture
in this dark

3:39am
how do i get
rid of the distance

between the title of a poem
and the line
where i say

i am mourning
the loss
of faith.

the order of things

and it happens
before the drums
before the collision in sunlight
before the day old salt on the lip of your collar
before the case of wine that takes all night to say goodbye

and it happens
before the flag rolled up in the corner
before the trapped water in motion
before the freckles greeting summer
before the used boarding pass folded for the past year

and it happens
before the hole in mom's eye
before the monotonous beat of good intent
before the arm becomes a twisted branch
before the heat on your face as you turn away

and it happens
before the incisions
before the scream in cement
before watching the fall
before wednesday agreements around a wooden table

and it happens
before the tongue touches lip
before the morning is called morning
before the question is forgotten
before taking the photo of a painting of your face

and it happens
before pink sheets
before cucumber vodka in the freezer
before the floor that can't hold the wheels in place
before her voice sounds like my name

and it happens
that the doctors can't explain anything
because i can't tell them the truth,
how this is what happens
to the ones that have been chosen—
the skin melting away
on the dog's leg
the hole in mother's eye
my brother's teeth turning purple
the mystery of my body
that stopped needing to create more life—
it is too easy to blame only
the abductions
and forget how we break
each time we return.

and it happens
before lemon juice dripped through fingers
before that second look as the car slowed
before the gush in the kitchen with feet spread apart
before the third step from the bottom as you reconsidered

and it happens

quiet
and an awkward glance out the window

while folding a pair of dirty pants,
misspelling love in secret
until it looked like
a finger held in the air
and curling
toward home.

the moment it begins

we sit,
my right knee two inches
from his left,
around his coffee table,
the one judy and i stole
after a night of bourbon
from a family loading a moving truck
in san clemente.

he taps the fingers
of his left hand
on the arm rest
of his recliner
as i try to manufacture
a desire
to hold
his hand.

and he turns away
from me,
points at his stomach
with his other hand,
and speaks a few words
to my reflection
on the television screen,
few words.

it begins with
questions
about the dog,

how she is coping
without her leg,
and i picture
that sunday
drunk on bottomless mimosas,
judy and i
standing at
the metal table
as the vet pointed
at the dog's leg,
the skin melting away
as we watched,
the dog shaking
from the memory
that all
of the cursed
have had embedded
into our skin.

i nod to him
when he is done,
to the him on the screen,
to the reflection
of my father
and he speaks
again,
this time about
the inevitable surprise
that we have been
waiting for.

i say okay
and i say, tell mom,
trying to buy time
to carry this word
he has given me,
cancer.

and there is
a noise i want
to make,
but i am 5 years old,
sitting on my parents' bed
and they are smiling
and they are telling me,
they say,
son, one day
we will die,
one day,
we will stop running,
one day,
we will release
each other.
and son,
they say,
you will have to learn
to recognize
happiness
on your own.
and they are laughing
until i am laughing,
and they are rolling
on their big bed,

pulling me into
the ether,
until i promise to sing,
until i promise them
a marching band,
until i run
to my room
and hide under my bed
and cry.

i grab his hand.
he still can't look at me
but i don't care
because
he has just spoken
the opening lines
of the final chapter
of our family
in this dark cold room
and it was transcribed
clumsily
in a poem,
this one,
by a son
that never wanted to understand
what it meant
to lose our past
and our future
for a chance
to touch
warm skin
in a present

that we were never
quite prepared
to meet.

tell me:

when the final chapter ends,
what will be different?
the morning light?
the roaches
on the edge of the sink?
the misplaced sock
sitting by the empty bottles?
when it ends,
won't the only regret
still be
standing on the balcony
afraid to knock,
hoping for the darkness
that shields me,
trying to stop my legs
from shaking
as i peeked in
to the promise
on the other side
of a large thin glass?

mercy and water

for the past year,
more than ever,
i've been trying to run away
from all things in my life,
wanting to create reasons
that can explain the way
my body has failed me.

years ago i ran all the way to new york,
ending up drunk on st. marks with a new tribe,
then leaving these strangers in bed
to walk in the rain
on 32nd and 3rd,
heading uptown then down
to that room where i left my bag
hanging on a metal chair,
surprised at the city,
how it keeps itself from getting lost
in the dawn breaking
between these two branches,
twisted and skinny,
pointing toward and away.

before that
was a house in the palisades
and another by the beach,
that one still haunted
by the owner's dead love,
and dark west l.a. bars
with sticky red booths
and blind promises exchanged through touch.

it's here again
and i can't quite handle
the slow way in which we are dying,
my family propped up
by secrets and scar tissues,
a yearlong charade of doctors and tests
that ends with me sitting
on an examining table,
the man with the polish name
telling me that he doesn't know
why bodies like mine stop.
"i can't explain it," he says.

and it leads to this:

walking out of another bar
into the night that is almost morning.
i put my hands in the pockets
of a $10 coat bought at a second hand store
on la brea,
unable to tell the time or the day,
how the past year has blurred
into an endless moment of regretting,

but the feet start to move faster without thought,
the memories in the body taking over,
mercy and water drops
on the curve of a side mirror—
the night and some path
toward that thing we call familiar,
a permanent forgiveness
like concrete and a tongue behind your ear—

wanting me to get there in time
to see her standing in front of the vanity,
rubbing scentless lotion
into her bare shoulders,
her speckled skin illuminated
by a small dim lamp
we found on the street.

hollywood hills

when i open my eyes,
it's the pale white mornings
that only come up in the hollywood hills.

there's a woman
hovering over me
as i try to not fall off the leather couch.

i look toward the sliding glass door
and notice the hardened candle wax
on the floor in the corner,
vaguely remember
kneeling next to it with a spatula,
scraping at it
until someone screamed
because i was messing up the wooden floor.

"you, give me a ride," the woman above me says
with an accent that i imagine is italian.
i rub my eyes, waiting for her face
to come into focus.

and i look down at the stain on my pant leg,
cum or spit or something else spilled in the night,
and nod, smiling, clarity setting in—

how the only proper way
to destroy myself
will be by saying yes,

to everything.

her journey

at the emergency room,
they kept using the word 'spontaneous'
and as i held her hand,
trying to stop myself from shaking,
i almost told her everything.
i got as far as saying that i was to blame
and staring at the floor.
but she said
i was being ridiculous,
that these things couldn't be my fault,
as my fingers gripped the steering wheel
of our car that wouldn't move
in the hospital garage,
calling my mother to tell her
and listening to her say nothing back.

it began with her
as the war broke out in korea,
the abductions.
she first saw the lights above her
as she hid in a row boat,
lying still and quiet on her back,
smiling at the way the colors in the sky moved,
and days later, when her father tied her to a chair
in the back room because he had to save his family
from the communist invasion
and one more girl was too much of a burden.
he told her to be quiet
but she wouldn't.
she screamed and she cried there alone.

they came, the ones from the lights in the sky,
untying her
and taking her over the ocean.

dad says it started for him around the same time
during the war that divided our homeland.
his father, my grandpa, the one with the belly
and the first one of us that made contact,
how he tried to buy time for his family
with a handshake deal while
my father, his second son,
carried his little sister
across the border in the night
to hide from the lights above.
sometimes i hear him angry
that we have been stuck in this life of running,
of hiding in the jungle in paraguay
as the invisible dragons circled
the air above chile,
of accepting our ability to sacrifice
friends and lovers to save ourselves.

it is strange.
the first they told me this
was on gramercy drive,
the living room with the gray carpet
of unit six, 950 gramercy drive,
my parents sitting on the couch,
how he leaned forward and tapped
mindlessly on the coffee table with his paint
caked fingers while my mother
started adding the pink yarn to the blanket—

standing in front of them
with my arms straight down to my sides
as he said,
son, in this life, you can't have friends
because you will have to lose them.

he never warned me about what happens
to our children,
how sometimes they are taken
before we can even know their skin,
or maybe i just hoped it would be different for mine.

it's been over two years now
since she's been gone,
taken on her journey from judy's womb.
spontaneous.

but last night,
she was here.
i rolled over on to my left
and in my half sleep
saw her standing five feet away.
she had grown,
in a pale dress and boots,
a jacket hugging tight around her shoulders.
she looked to be around ten years old
and in that moment i couldn't remember
how long ago was that day
that i can never escape.

she smiled, standing in a beam of light,
her hand lifting into the air,

to say hello, to say stop, to say stay,
and i bolted up,
waking up screaming,
hand reaching out across my wife's body,
to the light that filtered in through the window,

judy startled
wrapping her arms around me through instinct
as i began to wail at the fading light,
telling her
that i thought i heard
our baby say
goodbye.

the revision

i woke up terrified this morning,
how the ceiling was hanging up there
above us, still;
that ceiling and these still bodies,
mine, hers,
and these words,
so many falling short in more than five letters,
and dark that isn't dark,
and what i imagine will be branches outside
later on that will be swinging,
or swaying (i guess it's swaying when they are branches
or childhood hair or when we are dying in hunger
on the desert not many yards from a broken down buick,
beige diesel).
but there are stars, stars, yellow and rusted,
lifted with pale arms
on the other end of this stretch of floor
like suns, like pixelated reimaginings
of the moment he, dad, stood
on our roof between the door and the barbecue grill,
facing three-quarters away,
hands going into the pockets of his green pants,
saggy and folded over his shrinking body,
cowering from my screaming,
my screaming,
this rage when i learn
that he is failing at hiding how mom is dying in pieces,
when i hate everything that touches me,
warm skin then cold,
bones that bend without noise,

like him, the lips that whimper,
swaying swaying
like that thing in that place
outside of us,
ceiling and downstair cases
and white shelves of autumns
that leave while we disagree about progress;
the shadows that shifted an inch on the red tile floor
one summer in 79,
the buttons in my hand made by him,
the one in fear, failing,
the one with the pockets that hold and release,
still bodies of morning minus the inflection of her back
and the direction of bent will
and how the familiarity of this bed beneath us
means something that we are trying to embrace,
like morning light that is not light,
like a blue pencil held against the bridge
of a nose in laughter,
how i thought it was blue but i see that it is brown.
what else have i been wrong about,
what have i misjudged in the blinding light,
searched and found,
these things that i hold in sleep to keep them
from being born, unbirthing
my parents before it's too late, and how
i wake her from her sleep,
make her dress for an outing,
not the one next to me,
but hours after that one is gone,
how i tell her we will meet on the sidewalk of los angeles,
once empty, then filled, empty again

when it's early enough and cold enough,
and guide her to a table with the sun on her back,
sipping our drinks, splitting a sandwich
as she points at a large man and says that he,
that large man, can eat this whole sandwich but she can't;
counting the ingredients,
pausing at avocado,
as i check the time, desperate to revise this story
from the start before the end—
pointing at a brick in the wall,
tell her that it is a good brick,
that brick is what i like,
that brick can be used to build us,
that brick,
and she says, that is a good brick,
it is like the brick when i was young,
and i say, which brick is that,
and she says it's the brick before she got married,
before she had us, and pauses,
and she says, let's change the subject,
and i say, let's change everything,
and she says, how about that brick,
that brick i told you about,
the one that we lost before you came,
and i say, mouth full, i say, i know,
i think of that brick every week,
and how it reminds me of the one
that my wife carried,
this brick that we had planned to build walls on,
build a house,
a church,
a castle,

stairs.
i say i remember
but this is the moment,
i tell her,
mom this is the moment
where we can rebuild on this brick
like you told me when i was a child,
how i would one day save us all,
save us all,
and gave me a pen
and told me the stories
and put in my hands the brick
and said
go, go,
save us all, save us all,
and start it with a word
less than five letters
in the dark that holds the light
of the morning
to come.

today

another church,
this time in california,
says today is the day—
the apocalypse.
october 21, 2011.
it's not 9am yet.
this morning
the dog jumped up on the bed,
cone and all,
the first time she'd done it
since we were forced
to cut off her leg.

i am hungover
and my eyes are puffed up.
last night
after i got home from the bar,
i stood in the dark
and let my pants fall to the floor
and watched the neighbor
strip his date and fuck her awkwardly.
i don't know what i'm trying to force myself
to think right now.
the wife comes home
from her week in yosemite.
it was so dry the last time i visited it,
so much drier than
the first time my family made it up there
in 1980,
when my brother and i were still wearing matching shirts.

she will be home
and we will fumble our way
into making love
and she will tell me of the hikes
and the cold nights of sleep
and i will tell her
that today is the apocalypse
and that this time it is true
and i will tell her about my father,
the cancer they have found in his stomach,
and the way mom spoke to me on the phone yesterday,
having misheard me earlier
and thinking i would be there for dinner—
how she paused after the "oh, that,"
before she could say
"it is most likely cancer."

today begins
the last days of my family,
the secret of us
revealing through open windows
and dark corners;
how we were chosen
during the war
to die in a city of sunlight,
in the sequence that we all suspected—
father first
then mother after her blindness
then robert.

and i'd be left until the end,
not because i'm the youngest or the one that matters,

but only to document
the history we couldn't notice unfolding,
to figure out in uneven words
how to celebrate
these days
that we spent
waiting.

fissure

when we were in provence,
we walked on a road named after victor hugo.
it curved slightly and it was shaded by trees.
we stopped at a vendor's table
where an old man with a short gray beard
had many handmade sandals to sell.
judy tried them on,
the leather stiff around her feet,
knowing that with use,
the stiffness would give in to molding.
we bought a pair for her
and sat down to drink a bottle of wine
and eat duck and olives.
i took a picture of her,
a few pictures,
sitting across the table.

i took many pictures of the city
at each corner we came around,
of the signs that begin with rue and saint
and the sun that was different than the sun.
we were still a month away from coming home
and we'd come to provence
on buses and trains from barcelona,
across borders and languages,
first to marseille to eat bouillabaisse by the water,
only to be late by 2 hours for our reservation,
how i stood in front of the maitre d
pulling clean clothes out of my backpack
as he stared at me
trying to change into someone presentable.

reconstructing siberia

because this is a post-apocalypse story,
we will meet a survivor
crawling out from a fallen edifice,
jeans torn around the right knee.

he will hear some noise that connects
to a memory he can't quite identify,
not because he doesn't remember,
but because he has yet to learn how to place it
among the ruins at his feet.

the sky above him will be angry—
that is how the sky is described
at the time of armageddon—
and when he looks up at all that anger above him,
he will remember his father,
the man's left thumb wrapped in silver duct tape
holding together the piece he cut off
with a small saw.

but unexpectedly,
there will be a new tribe that finds him,
those that survived or were left behind,
and they will offer him a coat taken from a dead man
and one of them will say
that it would have been better
if he'd never woken up,
if none of them had ever woken up.

there will be metal signs dangling and creaking
above doors that no longer exist.
there will be the ash.
the ash will be there,
the ash from above that covers their skin
until it tastes like family,
until it tastes like holidays,
until it tightens around skin and veins.

and while trying to learn how to feel,
he will remember how he gave tours of los angeles,
the city where his grandfather was born,
where his father pointed at the street signs
to explain home to him as the boy rode shotgun
and stared at the length of his old man's finger
and how it curved sideways.

there will be a bus,
a shorty school bus on an empty school lot,
and the engine will turn over on the third try
and he will tell his tribe to get in.
this is my city, he will say,
this is my home.
and he will begin speaking about the gold rush
and how the streets burned before one april long ago
and when he sees the plaque engraved with i.n. van nuys,
he will smile and let them know they're in downtown.

he will take them on a tour.
he will take them on a journey.
he will tell them a story about the l.a. river,
how it wasn't a river at all,

but once,
that one time sitting on the edge with his grandfather
as they all waited for him to die,
everything about that moment,
including the river in front of them,
was real.

and at night he will get to make love
to the one that is even younger than himself,
the shy one that mistakes hopelessness for love,
and after the apocalypse,
there is always an epiphany,
one where our survivor discovers
that he has a special power.

and he will be afraid
when he learns that he has the power
as the keeper of memories
to rebuild it all, the entire city,
and so afraid, he will keep it to himself
until he lets it slip on a different night of sex,
and they will want him
they will want him to use this power
to rebuild their lives.
they will show him pictures of their yellow painted houses
and the park with the lake
and the coffee shop with the perfect ginger scones
and the highrises that were once
preserved through neglect
and the walk of fame
and the ferris wheel on santa monica pier
and the green langer's sign on 7th street.

he will do it all.
he will make it all rise from the ground,
and one night, unable to sleep,
he will grab the key to that short bus
and drive north to cesar chavez and head east
and he will stop when he is there,
at what once was the county hospital,
and he will begin
and he will raise up the emergency room and step inside
and he will place chairs
and he will sit in one of them for 14 hours
and on the television hanging near the ceiling,
a baseball game will begin and end,
and when it is time, when he is allowed,
he will go in the back and he will watch it again,
his daughter being taken into the atmosphere
on a ladder of light,
and he will watch his wife as she tries to smile
and he will think again
that the doctor looks younger than him
and of the day she moved here,
how they sat at a cafe on fairfax as the sun went down,
and she shivered
and said los angeles was the coldest city in the world

and he will get in the bus when it is done,
sit still,
notice his fingers wrapped around the steering wheel,
and tell himself
this is grace
this is grace
this is mercy

the bricks
the walls
the ceiling
this is grace
this is grace
the room
the house
the embrace
this is mercy
the sink
the slippers
the shelves—

the pain as salvation,
the end as the start,
an intersection that no longer exists—
this death that he has the power to recreate,
to hold on to eternally
like the warm fabric of his father's workpants,
clutched tight in his small hands
as he once fell asleep standing
on a crowded bus.

signals from space

it's always the sound
that touches me first
of the rain beginning to fall
outside.

this morning i looked out
into the courtyard of our apartment complex,
the brick red and the blue and the yellow
of the buildings
shining wet.

i put on my jacket
and my shoes,
giving the dog a treat
so she won't try to run out
into the hallway
and lose another leg.

i went outside,
started to walk north,
water sliding down my forehead,
over the freeway
toward chinatown.

there was music.
it was yo la tengo,
not that it matters,
but i am supposed to share details.

it has been
four years now.
it's hard for me to remember
the passing of the days,
already that long,
since she was taken,
our daughter.

judy left on my 41st birthday
to see her sister in charlotte,
to hold her new nephews,
twin boys named after drunken ancestors,
to pretend that she can still be a mother
even if it means returning home.

i am a cliché
crying in the rain
with drippy watermelon songs
loud in my ears
as pinwheels barely spin
in the entry ways of all
these chinatown storefronts.

looking up at the sky
with my eyes barely open,
sending messages into outer space,
hands cupped in the rain,
desperate to know
how to tell her
that i want to touch
this cold morning
with my tongue,

store my whispered secrets
in its skin
while waiting to catch the signals
she returns.

photo by Jamile Mafi

Chiwan Choi has had work published in ONTHEBUS, Esquire, and The Nervous Breakdown. His first collection of poetry, *The Flood* (Tía Chucha Press), was released in May 2010. He lives and works in Los Angeles.

CPSIA information can be obtained
at www.ICGtesting.com
Printed in the USA
FSOW02n2323120916
24942FS